CALIFORNIA MISSIONS

Discovering Mission San Juan Capistrano

BY JEANNETTE BUCKLEY

Cavendish Square

New York

Published in 2016 by Cavendish Square Publishing, LLC
243 5th Avenue, Suite 136, New York, NY 10016

Copyright © 2016 by Cavendish Square Publishing, LLC

First Edition

Website: cavendishsq.com

This publication represents the opinions and views of the author based on his or her personal experience, knowledge, and research. The information in this book serves as a general guide only. The author and publisher have used their best efforts in preparing this book and disclaim liability rising directly or indirectly from the use and application of this book.

CPSIA Compliance Information: Batch #CW16CSQ

All websites were available and accurate when this book was sent to press.

Library of Congress Cataloging-in-Publication Data

Buckley, Jeannette.
Discovering Mission San Juan Capistrano / Jeannette Buckley.
pages cm. — (California missions)
Includes bibliographical references and index.
ISBN 978-1-6271-3085-1 (hardcover) ISBN 978-1-5026-1217-5 (paperback) ISBN 978-1-6271-3087-5 (ebook)
1. Mission San Juan Capistrano—History—Juvenile literature. 2. Franciscans—California—San Juan Capistrano Region—History—Juvenile literature. 3. California—History—To 1846—Juvenile literature. I. Title.

F869.S395E339 2014
979.4'96—dc23

2014003915

Editorial Director: Dean Miller
Editor: Kristen Susienka
Copy Editor: Cynthia Roby
Art Director: Jeffrey Talbot
Designer: Douglas Brooks
Photo Researcher: J8 Media
Production Manager: Jennifer Ryder-Talbot
Production Editor: David McNamara

The photographs in this book are used by permission and through the courtesy of: Cover photo by Richard Cummins/Robert Harding/Getty Images; Frank Cortese/Shutterstock.com, 1; Ethel Davies/Robert Harding/Newscom, 4; Jessemonroy650/Ohlone hub(replica).jpg/Wikimedia Commons, 7; De Agostini/Getty Images, 8; Album/Florilegius/Album/SuperStock, 10; North Wind/North Wind Picture Archives, 12; © 2014 Pentacle Press, 13; © 2012 Pentacle Press, 16; © 2012 Pentacle Press, 17; © 2012 Pentacle Press, 19; Courtesy CMRC, 20; Fotosearch/Getty Images, 22; Iain Bagwell/Photolibrary/Getty Images, 24; North Wind/North Wind Picture Archives, 25; Peter Bennett/Ambient Images/Newscom, 29; Ken Wolter/Shutterstock.com, 30; Everett Collection/SuperStock, 31; © 2012 Pentacle Press, 32; Richard Cummins/Lonely Planet Images/Getty Images, 35; Eddie Brady/Lonely Planet Images/Getty Images, 36; Frank Cortese/Shutterstock.com, 41.

Printed in the United States of America

Contents

Mission San Juan Capistrano is a beautiful example of Spanish architecture, built by the men and women who lived there.

1
The Spanish Expand Their Empire

A SMALL CITY IN THE SAN JUAN VALLEY

Nestled in the San Juan Valley, close to the Pacific Ocean, is the city of San Juan Capistrano. Today this is a thriving place with shops, a downtown area, and many traditions. In its center sits a dust-colored brick wall that runs the length of a city block. Passing through the front gate, you arrive at one of the city's oldest landmarks, Mission San Juan Capistrano. Around the grounds are workshops and soldiers' barracks topped with red-tiled roofs. Trees and other plants grow abundantly. Under roof eaves perch mud nests built by the thousands of cliff swallows that live at the mission from March to October each year. Mission San Juan Capistrano was the seventh of twenty-one missions founded by the Spanish between 1769 and 1823 in California.

The Spanish and other European countries became interested in the land we now call California after Christopher Columbus discovered the New World (North America, South America, Central America and the Caribbean) in 1492. The king of Spain sent men to the New World to see what riches it offered, hoping to find gold, spices, and a western trade route to Asia.

RELIGIOUS FERVOR

Spain was also in a period of religious excitement. It had just expelled the Moors, who practiced Islam, after an 800-year occupation. In their excitement, the Spanish also wanted to share their religion with the inhabitants of the New World. The Spanish were Catholics and believed in the teachings of Jesus Christ and the Bible. They believed that only **Christians** went to heaven after they died. They wanted to **convert** the **indigenous people** to Catholicism to save their souls.

In those days, the term "Californias" was used to describe the area of land that includes today's state of California and the *Baja* Peninsula of Mexico. The southern portion of the Californias was named Baja, or lower, California, while the northern portion was called *Alta*, or upper, California. In 1542, the Spanish sent Juan Rodríguez Cabrillo to the Californias by ship to find a waterway that could serve as a trade route between Europe and Asia. Obviously, Cabrillo failed in this quest, as such a route does not actually exist. However, he did explore and map the **Alta California** coast, and discovered what would later be called San Diego Bay.

Sixty years later, when the Spanish king sent Sebastián Vizcaíno to find the water route, he also did not discover anything new. Spain then decided to stop sending explorers to that part of the world. It was not until 160 years later that another expedition would go to Alta California, this time to settle the land and build missions.

2
The
Acjáchemen

THE EARLY HISTORY OF THE ACJÁCHEMEN

The Native Americans living near where Mission San Juan Capistrano would be founded were mainly from the Acjáchemen

Most Native people lived in circular homes like this one.

Nation. When the Spanish arrived, they called these Native Americans "*Juaneño*," after the San Juan mission. Although there is no written history recording the early existence of the Acjáchemen, historians have pieced together information about the way they lived before the Spanish came through artifacts (such as tools, baskets, and weapons) and Acjáchemen legends that have been passed down from generation to generation.

The Acjáchemen lived in small villages, most of which were near a source of water. Each village was built around a central plaza. They shaped their homes in a cone by using a wooden form and **lashing** reeds and brush on top of it. The brush was attached in layers, like shingles on a house, to keep the inside dry. These homes were called *kiitcas*.

The Native people fished for food such as sharks, oysters, and clams.

IN TUNE WITH NATURE

The Acjáchemens' life was based on the natural world. Their homes, weapons, food, clothing, and religion were all dependent upon nature. Fending for themselves was essential to their survival, so they devised ways to get everything they needed from their environment.

The Acjáchemen men were responsible for hunting and fishing. Wearing little or no clothing during the summer months, they snared or trapped birds, squirrels, rabbits, mice, quail, and ducks. To trap an animal, the hunters sometimes set fire to the brush to force the animal to run right into the trap. They also hunted deer and antelope. They fished, caught sharks, and searched for oysters and clams.

The men made their tools and weapons from rocks, animal bones, shells, and sticks. Arrowheads and spear tips were forged from rocks and a naturally occurring glass called obsidian, which is hard and cuts easily. The Acjáchemen constructed bows from sturdy, flexible tree branches and bowstrings from vegetable stalks or animal sinew.

The women were responsible for gathering food and taking care of the children. Wearing apron-like skirts made out of hides, grass, or bark, they searched for edible plants and insects. They gathered cattail seeds, rushes, yucca stalks, wild plums, currants, celery, berries, seaweed, roots, and acorns. They tightly wove baskets out of reeds and used them for storing food, cooking, hauling water, and carrying children.

One of the major sources of nutrition in the Acjáchemens' diet was acorns, which were gathered in the fall. The women took special care in preparing them in order to remove a bitter acid that made them taste bad and could cause illness. After shelling the acorns, they crushed the nuts into flour. Then they cleaned the flour ten times. Once the flour was clean, the women used it to make soups, cakes, and breads.

SHAMANS HEALED THE SICK

Most Acjáchemen villages had a *shaman*, or medicine man, who used herbs and **rituals** to heal the sick. The Native Americans believed that shamans were able to communicate with spirits and were very important to the community. The canoe builders and chiefs of each village were also significant members of the community, and wore distinguishing long robes made of elk hides. In addition to dealing with community issues, the chief served as the group's religious leader.

The Acjáchemen religion was based on nature, and all of the Earth's creatures were significant and respected. The Acjáchemen believed in many gods and spirits, some which brought good fortune and happiness, while others were responsible for bad situations. To please their gods, the Acjáchemen held many rituals and ceremonies, which included dancing and singing. They used these ceremonies to acknowledge deaths, weddings, births, new chiefs, war, hunting trips, and initiations into adulthood for boys and girls.

Each Native group had different ways of celebrating, dancing, and singing.

3
The Mission System

A DIFFERENT WAY OF LIFE

Before starting missions in Alta California, the Spanish built similar religious communities across **New Spain**. These missions were set up in Central America, South America, and **Baja California** in the 1500s and 1600s. The government headquarters was set up in Mexico City, later the capital of New Spain.

Many indigenous people lived in New Spain. The Spanish built their missions near large Native American populations because they wanted to convert them to Christianity and teach them Spanish practices. The Spanish thought they could help the Native Americans by teaching them European trades, religion, and the Spanish language, which they believed to be superior.

The tribal people lived much differently than the Spanish did. They wore little or no clothing, while Spanish men wore shirts and trousers and Spanish women wore floor-length dresses. The Native Americans didn't have schools and couldn't read or write; many Spanish people attended school. They hunted game and gathered food from the wild, instead of farming crops. The Spanish considered the Native Americans to be beneath them, and thought of them as "savages," or like the animals of the forest.

The first religious order to set up missions in New Spain was the Jesuits. They taught the Native Americans about Spanish work methods and showed them how to care for livestock, plant and harvest crops, tool leather, work iron, make soap, and weave fabric for clothing. They also instructed them in the Catholic faith. In 1767, the Spanish took control of the missions in New Spain from the Jesuits, whom they believed were becoming too powerful. The **Franciscans** took their place. Soldiers then helped the Franciscan *frays*, or **friars**, build additional settlements in Alta California. They guarded the settlement and built presidios, or military fortresses, to keep the area safe from attack. There were four presidios in Alta California—at San Diego, Santa Barbara, Monterey, and San Francisco. They were strategically spaced so the soldiers could ride to whatever mission needed help.

The **missionaries** who joined in the expansion into Alta California planned for each mission to be run by two friars for about ten years.

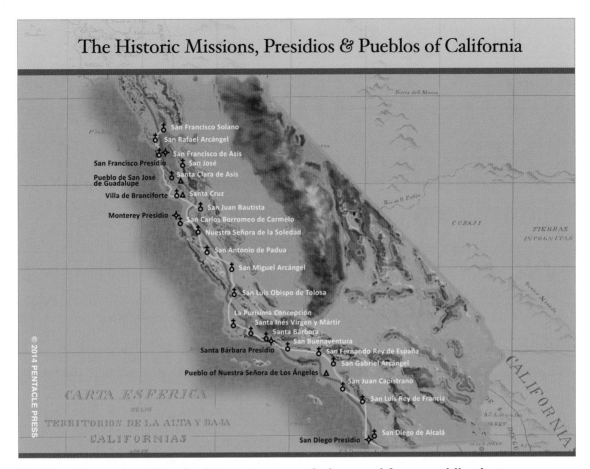

The Historic Missions, Presidios & Pueblos of California

San Francisco Solano
San Rafael Arcángel
San Francisco de Asís
San Francisco Presidio
San José
Pueblo de San José
de Guadalupe
Santa Clara de Asis
Villa de Branciforte
Santa Cruz
San Juan Bautista
Monterey Presidio
San Carlos Borromeo de Carmelo
Nuestra Señora de la Soledad
San Antonio de Padua
San Miguel Arcángel
San Luis Obispo de Tolosa
La Purísima Concepción
Santa Inés Virgen y Mártir
Santa Bárbara
San Buenaventura
Santa Bárbara Presidio
San Fernando Rey de España
San Gabriel Arcángel
Pueblo of Nuestra Señora de Los Ángeles
San Juan Capistrano
San Luis Rey de Francia
San Diego de Alcalá
San Diego Presidio

CALIFORNIA

CARTA ESFERICA
DE LOS
TERRITORIOS DE LA ALTA Y BAJA
CALIFORNIAS

Missionaries and soldiers built twenty-one missions and four presidios between 1769 and 1823.

The Spanish estimated that this was enough time to convert the indigenous people to Christianity and teach them trades. Then, operation of the mission would be turned over to the Native Amercians, who would become Spanish citizens. This process was called **secularization**. In this way, the Spanish gained control over new lands. They would gain citizens who had to pay taxes to Spain and would colonize the country for them, keeping it from other nations. Once a mission was secularized, the friars would travel to another area and help at other missions.

4
The Beginning of Mission San Juan Capistrano

FOUNDING FATHERS

The Spanish began settling Alta California in 1769, fearing that settlers from Russia and England would move in. They sent five expeditions of soldiers, missionaries, and Native Americans who had already been converted to Christianity from New Spain—what is today Mexico—with instructions to meet at San Diego. From there, they would construct a chain of missions along the Pacific coastline.

The expedition parties left New Spain under the command of Captain Gaspár de Portolá. Three parties sailed on the Pacific Ocean, while two traveled the 750 rocky and dusty miles up the Baja Peninsula. Portolá went by land, accompanied by Fray Junípero Serra. Many men died on the way, and one ship was lost at sea. Only about half of the 219 men who began the journey made it to San Diego.

Fray Serra was one of the two most important men in the founding of the missions. He was fifty-five years old when chosen by the Roman Catholic Church to be the mission president of Alta

California. Fray Serra founded nine missions in all. He made his headquarters at the second mission he founded, Mission San Carlos Borroméo del Río Carmelo, and tended to the missions for fifteen years. Fray Serra died on August 28, 1784, of general poor health.

The other important man was Fray Fermín Francisco de Lasuén. He was born on June 7, 1736, in Victoria, Spain. He arrived in New Spain in 1759. After Serra's death, Lasuén was chosen to head the mission chain. During the years from 1785 to 1803, he founded nine missions and encouraged the friars to teach new work methods. He made many improvements in the areas of construction, planting and harvesting crops, and raising livestock. Fray Lasuén died in 1803 at Mission San Carlos Borroméo del Río Carmelo, where he had also made his headquarters. He is buried in that mission's chapel alongside Fray Serra.

FOUNDING THE MISSION

As Fray Serra led a team of workers in building Mission San Diego de Alcalá, Portolá went off in search of the area an earlier expedition had chosen for Mission San Carlos Borroméo del Río Carmelo. Fray Juan Crespí, a former student of Fray Serra's, accompanied Portolá on the journey north.

On July 22, 1769, Crespí wrote in his diary about seeing Native Americans as they passed through the area where San Juan Capistrano would be founded. He noted that there were many trees and meadowlands, a valley, and plenty of water. The group named this lush spot Santa Maria Magdalena. Later, they also called it Wildfire Hollow because a brush fire had swept through the area. Crespí wrote that a boy and an infant had been burned in the fire. He **baptized** them on the spot because the children were near death.

CLOSING THE GAP

The first few missions established along the coast were far apart, so the Spanish began building to close the distance between them. The San Juan Valley was the midpoint between Mission San Diego de Alcalá and Mission San Gabriel Arcángel. This valley was chosen as the site for the seventh mission in the chain: Mission San Juan Capistrano.

In October of 1775, Fray Lasuén was part of an expedition that traveled to the site where Mission San Juan Capistrano was to be founded. In his group were Fray Gregório Amúrrio, a small squad of soldiers from the presidio of Mission San Diego de Alcalá, and two indigenous families originally from Baja California. They left Mission San Diego de Alcalá loaded with supplies for the new settlement, including cattle, grain, religious articles for the church, building materials, and tools. They arrived at the Acjáchemen village of Sajivit on October 30,

The Native people were upset by how they were being treated at the missions and retaliated against the soldiers and friars, as depicted above in an uprising at Mission San Diego de Alcalá.

Tensions at Mission San Diego de Alcalá halted construction at Mission San Juan Capistrano.

and selected a site nearby for Mission San Juan Capistrano. Fray Lasuén blessed the land, and the members of the expedition erected a cross on the new mission site.

The group then hauled timber to construct temporary shelters and a chapel. Eight days later, shocking news about Mission San Diego de Alcalá reached the party. On November 5, several hundred members of the Kumeyaay Nation, angered by beatings and other bad treatment, had attacked the mission. They stole religious articles from the church and set the mission buildings on fire. Several people were killed during the revolt, including the head missionary, Fray Luís Jaymé. The fighting stopped when the Spanish soldiers fired guns.

Fray Lasuén and his small group were all alone in the San Juan Valley, except for the Native Americans living in the Sajivit village. The Spanish didn't know how the local Acjáchemen would react to news of the revolt. The group didn't want to risk being attacked, so they buried the church bells, loaded up their belongings, and headed back to the presidio in San Diego.

5
The
Early Days

CROSS STILL STANDING

San Juan Capistrano was a mission in Alta California that was founded twice. After tensions between the Spanish and the Native Americans around the mission in San Diego quieted, the missionaries returned to the San Juan Valley and started the mission again. This time Fray Serra led the expedition, because Fray Lasuén had been sent to start construction of another mission. The mission president was pleased with the site, and called it a "place with abundant water, pasture, firewood, and timber."

Serra found that the cross erected by Lasuén's group was still standing. They dug up the bells and hung them from a tree. On November 1, 1776, Fray Serra conducted Mass and officially dedicated Mission San Juan Capistrano.

After the first two years, there wasn't enough water in the area to drink or to keep the crops growing, so the mission was moved near an Acjáchemen village where water was plentiful.

The mission complex was built to form a **quadrangle**, or a four-sided shape. The sides were not exact in length because the friars measured the length of each side by counting out paces, or

Sites for all of the missions were chosen by friars, often under the protection of soldiers.

number of steps, rather than using measuring instruments.

The friars and soldiers needed help building the mission. They attracted some of the local members of the Acjáchemen Nation by offering them food and trinkets such as glass beads. The Native Americans were also curious about the tools that the Spanish used, particularly axes made out of metal rather than stone. Eventually, some of the Acjáchemen began to help the missionaries.

In order to build permanent structures, the Spanish and the Acjáchemen gathered the materials they needed from the surrounding area. They chopped down trees from the nearby forests of pine and oak, cut the trees into planks and building supports, and hauled them to the construction site using *carretas*, or small wooden carts pulled by oxen or mules.

Wood for building was not abundant, so the missionaries showed the Acjáchemen how to make **adobe** bricks for the walls. The women and children were taught to mix mud, water, and straw by stomping it together with their feet. When the mixture was ready, the workers packed it into wooden molds to make bricks.

They placed the bricks in the sun to dry. The men placed the hardened bricks in layers to make the walls, securing them with mud.

Over the next several years, a church, living quarters for the missionaries, and dormitories for the Acjáchemen who lived at the mission were constructed. They built storage rooms and granaries for the wheat and barley they planted and harvested in fields near the mission. Weaving rooms, carpentry and blacksmithing shops, and soap-making and candle-making areas were also added to the mission. The workers dug wells in the courtyard and constructed an irrigation ditch from the Trabuco and San Juan Creeks to the mission, allowing water to flow into the crop fields. The first winery in Alta California was added in 1783. That year is the first for which detailed records still exist. Those records show that the mission had 430 cattle, 305 sheep, 830 goats, forty pigs, thirty-two horses, and one mule.

Friars at the missions taught neophytes how to make adobe bricks, farm, and care for livestock.

GROWING PAINS

The Serra Chapel, built in 1782, is the last remaining structure in which Fray Serra celebrated Mass. It is also the oldest building in California still in use. By 1796, it was too small to hold the number of neophytes—indigenous people who had converted to Christianity—living at the mission. To accommodate the 1,000 neophytes living at San Juan Capistrano in 1797, the friars decided to build a new church.

The new church would be constructed from stone instead of adobe. The neophytes mined the sandstone for the church from a quarry six miles away. Transporting it was hard. The big stones were loaded in oxen carts. Other stones were dragged by workers using chains or carried in nets by women and children.

The first stone was put in place in 1797. Isídro Aguilár, a master stonemason, arrived from New Spain in 1799 to make sure the new church would be strong and beautiful. Inspired by the churches of Europe, Aguilár designed a floor plan in the shape of a cross, and he carved graceful doorways and arches out of the stone.

The church took nearly nine years to build. In 1800, a small earthquake shook the area and set construction back. Many of the pillars and support beams had to be replaced. Aguilár himself died in 1803. When the church was finished in 1806, it measured 180 feet (55 meters) long and 40 feet (12 m) wide. The arched ceiling was five stories high and had seven domes. It could hold 1,000 neophytes. The friars held a two-day festival and invited all the important leaders of Alta California to attend the first religious service held in what they called the Great Stone Church.

Bells were very important to the mission. They told people when to pray, when to eat, and when to sleep.

6
Life at Mission San Juan Capistrano

CREATING A DAILY ROUTINE

Mission life was not always easy. The Acjáchemen living at the mission often voiced discontentment, although the attack on Mission San Diego de Alcalá was the only organized revolt in Alta California at that time. Neophytes were forced to obey a strict schedule of classes and work or face punishment. They could only leave for special reasons, such as monthly visits to their villages and special harvest times. Many Acjáchemen living at the mission were resentful of the missionaries' control over their lives.

At Mission San Juan Capistrano, residents woke to the sound of the mission bells. The bells rang at dawn signaling them to assemble and head to church for Mass, prayers, and lessons. After their religious duties, the neophytes were served a breakfast of *atole*, a mush containing corn or grain.

Following the morning meal, the missionaries gave out work assignments to the Acjáchemen men and women. In addition to cooking and tending to the children, the women made baskets in the Acjáchemen tradition. The Spanish showed them how to make soap and candles. The Spanish also instructed the women in weaving fabric using looms to make Spanish-style clothes for the men, children, missionaries, soldiers, and themselves. The Acjáchemen women also used this method to craft wool blankets.

LEARNING TO FARM

Acjáchemen men learned how to raise livestock, including cattle, sheep, horses, mules, and goats. Mission San Juan Capistrano established eight *ranchos*, or ranches, outside the mission complex. The ranchos included corrals, stables, sleeping quarters, and a chapel. The men who worked there were called *vaqueros*, meaning cowboys or ranch hands, and they tended to the animals that grazed on mission lands far away from the complex.

The Spanish also taught the Acjáchemen Spanish agricultural methods. They farmed wheat, barley, corn, and vegetables and planted orchards of peaches, walnuts, figs, red and green grapes, oranges, pears, olives, and date palms. The grapes were used to make wine, and the mission had an olive press to make olive oil.

Pozole was a popular dish to eat at the missions. It is still eaten today.

Some neophytes became vaqueros—the original cowboys—who took care of cows, sheep, and horses.

Olive oil was used as cooking oil, lamp oil, and as an item for trade. The mission also traded wine, soap, cloth, and hides with merchant ships for items such as musical instruments, furniture, and glass.

The Acjáchemen men were also taught trades at Mission San Juan Capistrano. The Spanish taught them **tanning** so they could make saddles, shoes, and hats. Blacksmiths from San Diego were brought in to show the men how to work the forge, a furnace for shaping metal. They learned how to make carretas, wagon wheels, locks, and keys.

After the morning work session, the Acjáchemen took a break for lunch. They ate *pozole,* a soup made of grain, vegetables, and a little meat, out of earthen jars. Then they took a *siesta*, a time for rest or a nap, and returned to work for a short period in the afternoon.

The day concluded with Mass and an *atole* supper. In the evening, the Native Americans were required to spend time in prayer, church instruction, and language lessons. Then they had some leisure time to dance, sing, and play games.

Mission life was especially confining for single girls and widows. They lived in dormitories, called *monjeríos*, and were kept separate from the other residents. Their quarters, as well as all mission doors, were locked at night to keep the neophytes in and others out. These women spent much time indoors.

BREAKING THE MONOTONY

On occasion, the Spanish held a *fiesta*, or festival, which broke up the monotony of mission life. Fiestas were held in honor of various saints, births, weddings, and important events in church history. The Acjáchemen also observed some of their traditional ceremonies. Although the friars often frowned upon these rituals, many allowed the ceremonies to occur so the Native Americans would be content and remain peaceful.

The missionaries were called on to perform many tasks. They taught the Acjáchemen about religion, crafts, farming, and ranching. They celebrated Mass and conducted baptisms, marriages, and funerals. They also had to keep the peace between the indigenous people and the soldiers.

The Spanish government required that the missionaries also keep detailed records of life at the mission, including agricultural productivity and the number of converts. Thanks to these records, we know that in the years 1783 to 1831 there were 234,879 bushels of wheat, barley, corn, beans, peas, lentils, *garbanzos* (chickpeas), and *habas* (broad beans) harvested at the mission. In 1812, 1,361 neophytes lived at the mission—its highest recorded population.

7
Decline and Hardship

HARSH TREATMENT

Mission San Juan Capistrano, along with other Alta California missions, experienced many hardships. Problems at the mission were caused by a number of things: cultural differences, diseases, pirate raids, and natural disasters. All troubles affected many people living there.

The Spanish and the Acjáchemen living at Mission San Juan Capistrano often clashed. Some of the Native Americans grew tired of mission life and wanted to return to their old ways. Sometimes they ran away because they weren't allowed to leave without permission. The Spanish hunted them down and brought them back to the mission. Other neophytes were often sent to round up those who were missing. The first time an escapee was caught, he was scolded. After that, runaways were often whipped or beaten. The Acjáchemen were also punished if the Spanish thought they weren't working hard enough, or if they stole something.

The Spanish soldiers were often harsh in their treatment of the neophytes. Throughout the mission system in Alta California there were reports that some Native Americans were beaten severely, and that some even died from these beatings.

Not all Acjáchemen wanted to join the mission. They didn't want to change their lifestyle or religion, and were upset that the Spanish had taken over their land. However, a number of the Acjáchemen at Mission San Juan Capistrano lived fairly peacefully because they were interested in learning skills and crafts.

Besides the two years of drought Mission San Juan Capistrano suffered early on, there were other natural disasters that took their toll. In 1812, just six years after the Great Stone Church was finished, a major earthquake rocked the mission. The disaster occurred in the morning of December 8, which is a special feast day in the Catholic Church, so the church was full. As the earth began to rumble, the mission bells rang wildly. Many of the neophytes were kneeling when the ground began to quake, and they couldn't get out of the church in time. Two boys were in the bell tower to ring the bells for Mass. They were killed when the tower crumbled. In all, forty people were crushed to death at the mission during the earthquake.

The church structure couldn't withstand the force of the earthquake. The heavy roof had split and collapsed, while the walls of the church were also cracked. Rather than trying to begin again, there was no effort to rebuild the Great Stone Church. Instead, services returned to the Serra Chapel.

The earth continued to rumble for a month, causing more damage to the mission buildings. Soon after, floods destroyed crops. The floods, which lasted for one year, caused more damage to the crumbling buildings. Disease plagued the livestock, and

Many neophytes who misbehaved were punished and sometimes imprisoned.

weeds got into the crop fields.

Disease also plagued the Acjáchemen, who were exposed to many European diseases they had never had contact with before, such as measles, chicken pox, smallpox, and tuberculosis. Since the indigenous people's bodies had not built up any resistance to such diseases, epidemics swept through all of the missions. In an epidemic in 1806, 100 Acjáchemen became very sick and died at Mission San Juan Capistrano.

One disease brought by the Spanish affected their ability to have children. In most of the mission areas, the death rate among the Native Americans grew to double the falling birth rate. This caused a rapid drop in the population of many Native American tribes.

UNHEALTHY LIFESTYLE

The Acjáchemen were used to living outdoors, so they suffered in the adobe dormitories, which were cramped, cool, and damp. The humid air made it hard for some people to breathe, and they

Ruins of San Juan Capistrano today.

became sick. In addition, the sanitation systems used by the missionaries attracted bugs and rats carrying germs and disease.

The Native Americans also suffered because of their change in diet. They were used to a balanced diet of grains, vegetables, fruit, fish, and lean animal meat. The Spanish brought cattle to Alta California, and introduced the Native Americans to milk. Lacking the **enzymes** to digest the milk, the Native Americans became ill.

Then, in 1818, pirates led by Hippolyte de Bouchard landed near Mission San Juan Capistrano and headed for the mission complex. Fray Gerónimo Boscano learned that the pirates were on their way, so he gathered the neophytes and left. The unopposed pirates stole wine and burned some of the mission buildings.

With fewer and fewer workers to fix the damage, Mission San Juan Capistrano, known as the Jewel of the Missions, fell into disrepair.

8
Secularization

MEXICO TAKES OVER

In 1810, the people of New Spain started a war with the Spanish government. For the eleven years of fighting, the Spanish government could not send enough supplies or money to the missions. Many people went hungry. Finally, in 1821, New Spain won independence and the nation of Mexico was born. Alta California and the missions now belonged to the new government.

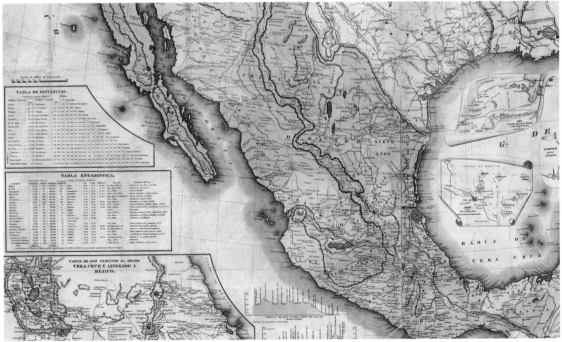

After 1821, Mexico gained the land that had once belonged to Spain, which included the California missions.

Friars, depicted here landing at Monterey, were removed from the missions during secularization.

Mexico wanted to end the mission system. In 1833, a law was passed by the Mexican government to begin the secularization of the missions. The next year an edict, or proclamation, was issued to speed up the process. When a mission was secularized, all the land, livestock, and buildings except for the churches were removed from the control of the Catholic Church.

Rather than turn the lands over to the Native Americans as the Spanish had intended, these laws gave the mission property to the Mexican government. Most of this property ended up in the hands of local landowners or Mexican officials. The Franciscans were removed and replaced by parish priests.

NATIVE CITY

Mission San Juan Capistrano, however, was different. Governor José Figueroa chose this mission as the site of a *pueblo de indios*, a Native American city with a municipal government. The mission buildings were converted into city administration buildings. The daily operations of the mission were turned over to the Acjáchemen neophytes to run, while a Mexican official was placed in charge of the overall operation.

Within the first couple of years, the pueblo de indios collapsed. The Acjáchemen complained to Governor Figueroa that the official in charge was using their labor for his personal gain. They also reported that he illegally sold off a lot of the land, as well as the livestock and several buildings, to settlers. As a result, many of the indigenous people left the pueblo and took jobs in Los Angeles as vaqueros, cooks, or factory workers. When the mission was secularized in 1833, there were still 831 Acjáchemen living there. By 1840, there were only about 100 left living at the mission.

Alta California as a region saw great change as well. In the 1840s, United States citizens began settling in California and petitioned their government to make California a state. America went to war with Mexico in 1846, and in 1848 won possession of the land. Gold was discovered in 1848. In 1850, California became the thirty-first state. And, in 1865, President Abraham Lincoln signed the order returning Mission San Juan Capistrano to the Catholic Church.

9
The
Mission Today

A NEW TOWN GROWS

As years passed and the 1860s arrived, Mission San Juan Capistrano was suffering. Settlers, wishing to build homes and businesses, had stolen most of the bricks, tiles, and wood that had made up the mission walls. The mission was bare. Sadly, it continued to deteriorate until the 1890s.

However, the town around the mission grew rapidly. The California Central Railroad was built in 1887, and San Juan Capistrano served as the halfway point between San Diego and Los Angeles. Local farmers could easily transport their oranges, walnuts, barley, and olives to large cities using the train. By the beginning of the twentieth century, the town was thriving.

In 1895, the Landmarks Club of California spearheaded an effort to restore the mission. They raised money to purchase supplies and made some of the repairs, including placing a roof on the Serra Chapel. In 1910, Father John O'Sullivan took over restoration of the mission. He returned the chapel to full service by 1918. The work was publicized in the *Los Angeles Times*, which drew the attention of the Hollywood crowd. In 1939, Leon René composed the hit

Preservation work on Mission San Juan Capistrano was started by Father John O'Sullivan in 1910 and continues today.

song, "When the Swallows Come Back to Capistrano." By the 1940s, the mission had become a popular tourist spot.

RESTORATION CONTINUES

Mission San Juan Capistrano is an important historical site and is still being restored. Ten acres (4.06 hectares) of the original mission complex have been turned into an outdoor museum. Now known as the Mission San Juan Capistrano Historic Landmark and Museum, it offers educational classes about California's history to visitors, including school groups.

Visitors can tour the grounds and restored buildings. They can peek into a kiitca like those the Acjáchemen lived in before the Spanish arrived, or they can see the factories where the mission workers made candles, soap, olive oil, and wine. Other things to see at the museum include the original mission bells, cemetery, Serra Chapel, soldiers' barracks, jail, and the ruins of the Great Stone Church destroyed in the earthquake of 1812. The museum also features exhibits on tools, baskets, wine making, plants and herbs, and the famous swallows that still build their nests on the mission grounds.

The mission system's influences on the state of California can still be seen today. For example, methods of farming and ranching that the friars taught to the Native people are now major parts of California's industry. Many crops begun at the missions, such as olives, grapes, and oranges, are still produced. Spanish architecture still flourishes on the buildings in cities. While the missions changed the lifestyle of many, which should always be remembered, they also helped make California what it is today.

Mission San Juan Capistrano offers tourists much to see and do, including walking around these reconstructed ruins.

10
Make Your Own Mission Model

To make your own model of Mission San Juan Capistrano, you will need:

- Foam Core board
- X-ACTO® knife
  (ask for an adult's help)
- ruler
- glue
- tape
- pencil
- modeling clay
- toothpicks
- bells
- cream, green-colored paint
- red felt
- cardboard
- colored construction paper

DIRECTIONS

Adult supervision is suggested.

Step 1: To make the base, cut a Foam Core board rectangle that measures 20" × 15" (50.8 cm × 38.1 cm). Paint with green paint. Let dry.

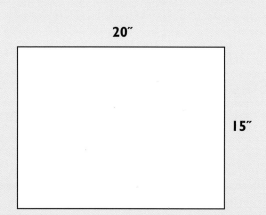

20″

15″

Step 2: To make the workshop, cut a Foam Core board rectangle that measures 17″ × 2.5″ (43.1 cm × 6.4 cm).

Step 3: Take the rectangle and draw a faint line with pencil 7″ (17.8 cm) from the edge. Bend the board along this line.

Step 4: Cut a 13″ × 2″ (33 cm× 5.1 cm) piece. Cut arches in the bottom. Draw a line 5″ (12.7 cm) from edge. Bend the board along this line.

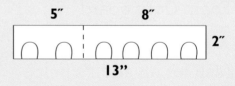

Step 5: To make the sides of the workshop, cut two 2″ × 3.5″ (5.1 cm × 8.9 cm) house-shaped pieces.

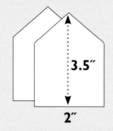

Step 6: Glue together front, back, and side walls to make an "L" shape. Attach to base.

Step 7: To make the church, cut a 17″ × 14″ (43.2 cm × 35.6 cm) Foam Core rectangle. Cut a 5″ × 5″ (12.7 cm × 12.7 cm) square out of each corner, leaving a plus sign.

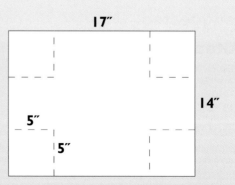

Step 8: Fold the sides of the plus sign up to form a box. Tape sides on the inside of the box shape.

Step 9: Turn the box shape over and attach to base.

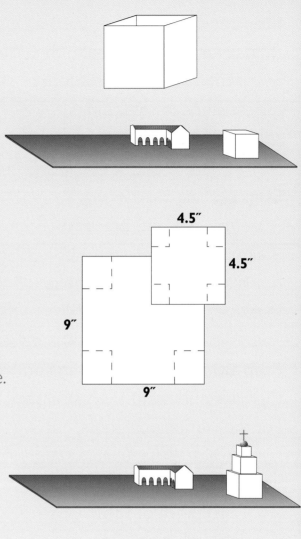

Step 10: To make the tower, make a 9" × 9" (22.9 cm × 22.9 cm) square and a 4.5" × 4.5" (11.4 cm × 11.4 cm) square. Cut four 3" (7.6 cm) corners out of the larger square. Cut four 1.5" (3.8 cm) corners out of the smaller square. Repeat the folding instructions followed for the church. Add a ball of clay to the top of the tower. Stick a toothpick cross in the clay ball.

Step 11: To make the soldier's quarters, cut out two 5" × 2" (12.7 cm × 5.1 cm) pieces and two 2" × 3.5" (5.1 cm x 8.9 cm) pieces with triangular house tops from the Foam Core board. Cut doors from one 5" × 2" (12.7 cm × 5.1 cm) piece.

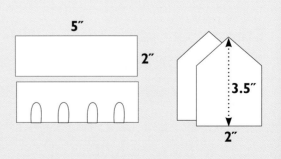

Step 12: Glue together pieces to make a house. To make the friars' quarters and the kitchen, repeat steps for making soldiers' quarters.

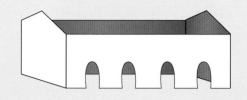

Step 13: Cut out a 4" × 2" (10.2 cm × 5.1 cm) piece to make the bell wall. Cut out holes for bells and glue bells in place.

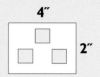

4"

2"

Step 14: Place the buildings on the base and paint them cream. For the workshops' roofs, cut out a 7" × 3.75" (17.8 cm × 9.5 cm), and an 8" × 3.75" (20.3 cm × 9.5 cm) piece of Foam Core board. Bend each rectangle in half the long way.

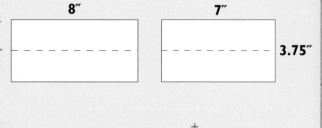

8"

7"

3.75"

Step 15: Cut out three 5" × 3.75" (12.7 cm × 9.5 cm) rectangles for the roofs of the soldiers' quarters, friars' quarters, and kitchen. Fold them in half.

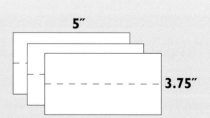

5"

3.75"

Step 16: Attach roofs to the buildings and cover with red felt. Decorate the mission with flowers and trees which you can make out of colored construction or tissue paper.

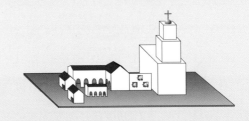

The model of Mission San Juan Capistrano when completed.

Key Dates in Mission History

1492	Christopher Columbus reaches the West Indies
1542	Cabrillo's expedition to California
1602	Sebastián Vizcaíno sails to California
1713	Fray Junípero Serra is born
1769	Founding of San Diego de Alcalá
1770	Founding of San Carlos Borroméo del Río Carmelo
1771	Founding of San Antonio de Padua and San Gabriel Arcángel
1772	Founding of San Luis Obispo de Tolosa
1775–76	Founding of San Juan Capistrano
1776	Founding of San Francisco de Asís
1776	Declaration of Independence is signed

1777	Founding of Santa Clara de Asís
1782	Founding of San Buenaventura
1784	Fray Serra dies
1786	Founding of Santa Bárbara
1787	Founding of La Purísima Concepción
1791	Founding of Santa Cruz and Nuestra Señora de la Soledad
1797	Founding of San José, San Juan Bautista, San Miguel Arcángel, and San Fernando Rey de España
1798	Founding of San Luis Rey de Francia
1804	Founding of Santa Inés
1817	Founding of San Rafael Arcángel
1823	Founding of San Francisco Solano
1833	Secularization Act passed by Mexico
1848	Gold found in northern California
1850	California becomes the thirty-first state

Glossary

adobe (uh-DOH-bee) Sun-dried bricks made of straw, mud, and sometimes manure.

Alta California (AL-tuh ka-luh-FOR-nyuh) The mission area today known as the state of California.

Baja California (BAH-ha ka-luh-FOR-nyuh) The Mexican peninsula directly south of the state of California.

baptize (BAP-tyz) To perform a sacrament marked by ritual use of water that makes someone a member of a Christian community and cleanses the person of his or her sins.

Christian (KRIS-chun) Someone who follows the Christian religion, or the teachings of Jesus Christ and the Bible.

convert (kun-VERT) To change religious beliefs.

enzyme (EN-zym) A chemical substance in animals and plants that helps to cause natural processes such as digestion.

Franciscan (fran-SIS-kin) A member of a Catholic religious group started by Saint Francis of Assisi in 1209.

friar (FRY-ur) A brother in a communal religious order. Friars can also be priests.

indigenous people (in-DIJ-en-us PEA-pel) People native born to a particular region or environment.

lash (LASH) To tie or fasten together with a rope.

missionaries (MIH-shuh-nayr-ees) Men and women who teach their religion to people with different beliefs.

New Spain (NOO SPAYN) A region colonized by Spain that included, among other areas, what is now Mexico as well as the states of Florida, Texas, Arizona, New Mexico, California and Nevada.

quadrangle (KWAH-drayn-gul) The square at the center of a mission that is surrounded by four buildings.

ritual (RIH-choo-uhl) A ceremony marking an event.

secularization (sehk-yoo-luh-rih-ZAY-shun) A process by which the mission lands were made to be nonreligious.

tanning (TA-ning) Turning animal hides into leather by soaking them in a special liquid.

Pronunciation Guide

Acjáchemen (ah-HA-sheh-men)

atole (ah-TOH-lay)

carretas (kah-RAY-tahs)

fiestas (fee-EHS-tahs)

fray (FRAY)

kiitcas (KEE-shas)

monjerío (mohn-hay-REE-oh)

pozole (poh-SOH-lay)

pueblo de indios (PWAY-bloh DAY IN-dee-ohs)

ranchos (RAHN-chohs)

siesta (see-EHS-tah)

vaqueros (bah-KEH-rohs)

Find Out More

For more information about Mission San Juan Capistrano and the missions of California, check out these books and websites:

BOOKS

Bibby, Brian. *The Fine Art of California Indian Basketry*. Berkeley, CA: Heydey, 2013.

Lemke, Nancy. *Southern Coast Missions of California*. Minneapolis, MN: Lerner Publishing, 2008.

Gibson, Karen Bush. *Native American History for Kids*. Chicago, IL: Chicago Review Press, 2010.

Rosinsky, Natalie M. *California Ranchos*. Edina, MN: Capstone Publishers, 2006.

WEBSITES

California Mission Foundation

www.californiamissionfoundation.org

Find quick and easy facts about the missions and discover more about the organization that preserves and protects the missions today.

California Missions Resource Center

www.missionscalifornia.com

Interact with a mission timeline, videos, and photo gallery and unlock key facts about each mission in the California mission system.

A Virtual Tour of California Missions

missiontour.org/sanjose/history.htm

Understand key events in the mission of San José by reading this detailed timeline of the mission's history.

Juaneño Band of Mission Indians Acjáchemen

juaneno.com

Read about history, beliefs, and culture of the Juaneño Band of Mission Indians Acjáchemen Nation today.

Ranchos of California

cluster3.lib.berkeley.edu/EART/rancho.html

Discover all about historical information on the ranchos of California, courtesy of the UC-Berkeley Library.

Index

Page numbers in **boldface** are illustrations.